GOD IS IN THE HALLWAY
An Equipping Devotional for
Christian Educators

Angie Burgin Kratzer

ISBN-10:1536836257
ISBN-13: 978-1536836257

DEDICATION

This book is dedicated to all shield-bearing educators.

CONTENTS

ACKNOWLEDGMENTS

Many thanks to David and Michele Mallard for being my theological sounding board and to Ann Hornack and Melinda King for giving home school and public-school perspectives on the text. To Yogi Collins, my B.E.A.N. prayer warriors, the SAALAD girls, and my family: I thank you for always cheering me on.

ABOUT THIS BOOK

Each classroom, each school, each office, and each board meeting is a battleground. This twelve-week devotional is designed for individuals or small groups of educators who want to glorify God and get equipped for the fight of their lives. We're powerless without an understanding of who God is, who we are to him, and what weapons we already have for the hardest job there is.

This set is comprised of five-day sets of readings and exercises. The materials can easily be switched up and re-ordered or completed in a day or two if that is the user's preference.

Day 1 (Monday): Devotional Reading
Day 1 always features a short essay on a particular truth about God and our relationship with him.

Day 2 (Tuesday): Action
Day 2 applies the Day 1 reading to our daily lives as educators.

Day 3 (Wednesday): Scripture Memorization
Day 3 introduces relevant scripture and suggests strategies for memorizing it. Most verses are given in three different Bible versions. The New International Version, English Standard Version, and King James Version are used most often.

Day 4 (Thursday): Scripture Study
Day 4 includes historical context for the Day 3 scripture and offers inductive study questions for meditation and application.

Day 5 (Friday): Reflection
Day 5 is for processing your own thoughts, God's revelation, the confession of sin, and any changes you need to make in your thinking or behavior.

SMALL GROUP TIPS

- Gather a group of three to ten believers.

- Pick a time to meet weekly (before or after "clocked" hours) and choose someone to be the facilitator.

- Make a "What happens here, stays here" agreement.

- Open in prayer each time you meet. Allow for silent time so that participants may confess sin, clear their minds, etc. Pray for the Spirit to encourage, teach, and convict. Pray for protection from the enemy.

- When together, move through each day in order and discuss what you learned. (The facilitator can make each meeting unique with a variety of strategies.)

- Here's one way the discussion might work:

  - Day 1: Each person identifies and shares a sentence, phrase, or word that spoke to him or her. Volunteers offer up their choices and explain.

  - Day 2: The work required for this day may be a bit personal for sharing, but the facilitator can ask if anyone has something that is edifying for the group.

  - Day 3: Each person says or writes the memorized verse. (The group members decide the level of accountability beforehand.)

  - Day 4: Spend some time answering the questions, discussing different translations, and applying the scripture.

  - Day 5: Again, this day may be too personal to share, but the ideal would be group members feeling safe enough to tell everyone what they have learned throughout the week and get feedback.

GOD IS IN THE HALLWAY

WEEK I, DAY I
God is in the Hallway

Grocery stores. The right girl. Traffic jams. Public restrooms. Graduation. The sale of a house. Proposals. Dawdling preschoolers. Pregnancy. The phone. The dentist's waiting room.

We do a lot of waiting.

I didn't marry until I was 33. There were good men but no one who loved Jesus more than he loved me. So, I chose loneliness over regret. And waited. And waited. By the time Stan and I found each other, I knew who I was as a woman and as a daughter of God.

For ten years, we struggled with infertility. After all the tests, shots, pills, and procedures, I can say with certainty that there is no longer wait than the three minutes it takes for that little line to show up on a pregnancy test. That time never speeds up, even when you've taken one every month for *years*. After a heartbreaking miscarriage and an adoption that fell through one week before the baby was born, we stopped. We decided that pursuing an international adoption of an older orphan was the way to go, and on a Tuesday night we were paper ready for a child from Uganda. I sealed the envelope and crawled into bed. That night, we prayed and let go of ever being the parents of an infant. Grief put us to sleep.

The next afternoon, a childhood friend called to ask if we still wanted to adopt. For twenty years, she had been a sonographer specializing in obstetrics, and she had a patient who was unable to parent her son. This young married couple who already had three children knew they could not provide for a fourth. Ten days later, I was holding that woman's hand as she gave birth to Samuel, our beautiful, multiracial, smart, active boy. Preparing for Uganda prepared me for him.

God is in the waiting. It's not at the end of the journey that we experience the power of trusting Jesus; it's in the middle of the trip. Noah didn't learn to trust God when the waters dried up. Moses didn't learn to trust God when the Israelites reached the Promised Land.

I'm a high school teacher. For my students, life happens in the hallway between classes. It is there that they learn how to do relationships, how to trust, whom to trust, and how to wait—for love, for acceptance, for approval. God is in the midst of them, the One who can be trusted, the One who loves and accepts them as they come to him.

God is in the hallway.

WEEK 1, DAY 2
God is in the Hallway: Certainty and Uncertainty

List the periods of waiting you have during a typical day. Consider your morning routine, commute, the copier line, etc.

What are you waiting for? Friday? The last day of school? Retirement? The sale of a house? List a few things you are fairly certain will happen but seem to be taking their time.

What else are you waiting for? A spouse? The money to buy a house? Permission to transfer schools? Adoption? The cure for an illness? List a few needs and desires you have that may or may not be fulfilled.

Clear 20 minutes in your day to pray through these lists. Ask God to direct you during your times of waiting. Take to him your anxiety about your unmet needs and unfulfilled desires. Ask for the Holy Spirit to show you where God wants to stretch or challenge you.

WEEK I, DAY 3
God is in the Hallway: Scripture Memorization

Psalm 27:14

ESV

Wait for the Lord; be strong, and let your heart take courage; wait for the Lord!

NIV

Wait for the LORD; be strong and take heart and wait for the LORD.

KJV

Wait on the LORD: be of good courage, and he shall strengthen thine heart: wait, I say, on the LORD.

Choose one version of the verse above and write it here.

Create a diagram below depicting the three sections of this verse.

WEEK 1, DAY 4
God is in the Hallway: Scripture Study

Write Psalm 27:14 here.

Context
Scholars agree that David wrote this psalm, but they don't agree on the event that inspired it. Christian theologians tend to think David wrote it before he was crowned, but Jewish theologians place it near the end of King David's life.

Real Psalm 27 in its entirety.
What is David's perspective of God? What character traits of God does David express in the psalm?

Language
Two Hebrew words that are often translated as "wait" are *qavah* and *yachal*. Both have several definitions, but one common meaning is to "hope, expect, look eagerly." *Qavah* also means "to bind together," and *yachal* has been translated as "trust" and "wait in hope."

How does your understanding of these two Hebrew words contribute to your understanding of the verse and the psalm as a whole?

WEEK 1, DAY 5
God is in the Hallway: Reflection

Write Psalm 27:14 here.

How has your understanding of waiting changed this week?

Image a parent whose child is at war or a senior who cannot go to college without the scholarships for which he has applied. Think back to a time in your life when you were close to losing hope while waiting. Briefly describe the situation. Where were your mind and heart during that time?

In what areas have you realized that you are expecting satisfaction from reaching the end rather than experiencing Christ in the journey?

WEEK 2, DAY 1
Simple and Clear

Before we really start chewing on the truths that equip us to serve Christ in the classroom, let's begin with THE TRUTH, the clear, simple, logical, and perfect Gospel.

God created this world, its animals, its plants, its people, food, sex, pleasure, and laughter. He was in a perfect, loving relationship with his creation until the people he created walked away from all of this goodness and rebelled against him by choosing to disobey. That rebellion, pushback, and the inclination toward it is ingrained in humans, and many call it our "sinful nature." We have a proclivity toward it. Need evidence? You don't have to teach a three-year-old kid to lie. She just does it. When I wrote the first draft of this essay, a young man had just shot 49 people at a night club in Orlando, Florida. A man was just released from prison—31 years of it—after it was discovered that he did not commit the rape he was convicted of perpetrating. Parenting wasn't meant to be so hard.

We were not designed for hate. Systems run by humans fail. We are separated from God.

We. Are. Broken. As a species, we are not evolving morally; it's not getting better. God sees us, hears us, and is active in the lives of his creation even though the creatures continue to disobey. He watches while his beloved children use religion, food, money, possessions, and even altruism to fill the hole left by his absence. These scenes playing out before him grieve him just as they would a parent. But this parent isn't helpless. He has provided a way to reconcile with his children.

It's simple, really. According to God's Word, the Bible, sin has to be punished, and the punishment is death, both physical and spiritual. It is permanent, eternal separation from God. Someone has to pay. Because God longs to be back in relationship with us, he became a man and died so that we wouldn't have to. Jesus Christ, God in the flesh, was killed through a Roman form of capital punishment, crucifixion, an excruciatingly slow way to die. The sin of all mankind was on him when he died. He paid the price. Done. With his last breath, he gasped, "It is finished." Three days later, he rose from the dead in victory over death itself. Dying wasn't enough; he had to win a larger victory—the greatest victory—for life.

That life with God, that *reconciled* life with God, is now ours for the asking, and it begins with a conversation in which you admit your sin (name them if you can), ask for forgiveness, and trust God to do a better job of directing your life than you have.

WEEK 2, DAY 2
Simple and Clear: Losing Sight

I've recently discovered divided plates with pictures on them. For my entire life, I have struggled with overeating, and I now meet regularly with a registered dietician to work on my habits. She has on her desk a smallish plastic plate divided into sections for fruits and vegetable, carbs, and protein. I tend to use big plates, on which I pile as much of a particular food as I want. With a smaller bariatric version, I can visualize the proper portion size and serve myself accordingly. Chicken breast=deck of cards. Mashed potatoes=half a cup. Salad=half the plate. By constantly reminding myself of what a portion should be, I can keep my eating in line. If I don't, things get all wonky, and I give myself two cups of mashed potatoes.

The same concept is true for the Gospel of Jesus Christ. We have to keep reminding ourselves of the truth or we lose sight of its simplicity and beauty. Otherwise, we're complicating it with debates about the tribulation and immersion.

In the course of a day, what are some ways you can remind yourself of the Gospel?

In the space below, rewrite the Day 1 explanation as you would tell it to a six-year-old child. It's that simple!

WEEK 2, DAY 3
Simple and Clear: Scripture Memorization

Romans 3:23-25a

NIV
[. . .] for all have sinned and fall short of the glory of God, and all are justified freely by his grace through the redemption that came by Christ Jesus. God presented Christ as a sacrifice of atonement, through the shedding of his blood—to be received by faith.

NASB
[. . .] for all have sinned and fall short of the glory of God, being justified as a gift by His grace through the redemption which is in Christ Jesus; whom God displayed publicly as a propitiation in His blood through faith.

KJV
[. . .] for all have sinned, and come short of the glory of God; being justified freely by his grace through the redemption that is in Christ Jesus: whom God hath set forth to be a propitiation through faith in his blood [. . .]

Choose one version of the verse above and write it here.

WEEK 2, DAY 4
Simple and Clear: Scripture Study

Write Romans 3:23-25a here.

Context

The Apostle Paul wrote this letter to a mixed group of Jewish and Gentile believers in Rome. This church had probably been around for several years, but Paul had never visited. Word reached Paul that the Gentiles were being pressured to comply with Jewish traditions and observances, including circumcision.

Source: Kulikovsky, Andrew S. "The Historical Context of Paul's Letters to the Galatians and Romans." kulikovskyonline.net. 8 Apr. 1999. Web. 19 Jul. 2016.

Using the graphic organizer on the next page, identify four components of the Gospel found in these verses.

Romans
3:23-25a

WEEK 2, DAY 5
Simple and Clear: Reflection

Write Romans 3:23-25a here.

Why is it important for you personally to remind yourself of the Gospel frequently?

Why is it important for you professionally to remind yourself of the Gospel frequently?

Which element of the Gospel do you want or need to study further in order to explain it clearly?

      Mankind's condition

      The penalty for sin

      Jesus' substitutionary sacrifice

      A person's response in faith

How will you go about this study?

WEEK 3, DAY 1
How God Sees You

Our sun is a star, one of about 200 billion in our own Milky Way galaxy. In the universe we can see with our telescopes, there are *billions* of galaxies, perhaps as many as 100 billion. That's 100,000,000,000.

The God who made that expanse knows that you love syrup on your bacon.

A little crustacean, the peacock mantis shrimp, has the most powerful punch in the animal kingdom, enough to break through reinforced aquarium glass. In 2012, *The New York Times* ran an article about the little beast whose "club is composed of a highly crystallized form of calcium phosphate, the same mineral found in bones. This gives it a high compressive strength. Under that are rods of material called chitin, stacked at different angles, which helps prevent fractures from growing."

The God who designed that creature knows what you dream about. HE *KNOWS* YOU. He knows how many hairs you have on your head. HE *MADE* YOU. He carefully knit you together in your mother's womb.

With all your crap, all your junk, all your sin, all your unspoken hatred, all your addictions, all the times you succumbed, all your vanity, all your past, all your cheats, all your ugly, HE *WANTS* YOU. HE *CHOOSES* YOU.

Hear this: GOD *ADORES* YOU. Once you confessed your sin and separation from him and accepted his forgiveness by faith, HE *ADOPTED* YOU. Jesus took on your sin when he died; when God looks at you, the sin isn't there. To him, you are clean and unblemished.

But don't get him wrong. God doesn't play around; he is jealous for your heart, your time, your attention, and your obedience as any parent would be. He chose to use the father metaphor to help us understand his attitude toward us, but the metaphor is flawed because we are. Like mothers and children, fathers lose sight of their priorities, but God does not. Fathers can be rash, but God is not. Fathers can give up on us, but God will not. He chose to describe himself as the father because he is tender toward you, wants to give you good things, longs to protect you from harm, craves time with you, and calls you his own. You are his own, beloved.

How God Sees You: Living it Out

Describe your father's personality. If he has been absent for whatever reason, that's significant. If you never knew him or have spent very little time with him, what are your impressions?

Our view of God, who revealed himself to us as masculine, can often be skewed by our view of our earthly father. Now describe God's character.

Who you imagine God to be will directly impact how you see yourself and how you operate in his kingdom. He is fully just and fully merciful. With an unbalanced view of those two traits, your projection of the character of God to your peers and students can be cold and dogmatic or loose and permissive. One the scale that follows, draw a dot where you find your own beliefs about God.

JUST   MERCIFUL

An educator has the unique position of having a captive audience who will see and hear about a relationship with God. What will your captive audience see and hear from you before ever learning that you're a believer? Does your school life reflect a true, balanced, scripturally accurate view of who God and is and who you are to him?

WEEK 3, DAY 3
How God Sees You: Scripture Memorization

1 John 3:1

ESV
See what kind of love the Father has given to us, that we should be called children of God; and so we are.
NIV
See what great love the Father has lavished on us, that we should be called children of God! And that is what we are!
KJV
Behold, what manner of love the Father hath bestowed upon us, that we should be called the sons of God [...]

Choose one version of the verse above and write it here.

Memorization Tip:
Put this week's scripture card in your pants pocket. Every time you're in line, waiting at a stoplight, or seated before a meeting starts, pull out the card.

WEEK 3, DAY 4
How God Sees You: Scripture Study

Write 1 John 3:1 here.

Context

Although he is never mentioned by name in the letter, the Apostle John is considered by most scholars to be the author. This is the same follower of Christ who wrote the fourth Gospel, the Book of John. Much of the content of the text counters Gnosticism, a belief system that included the idea that Jesus was not God incarnate. In other words, some believed he was fully God but not fully human.

Read all of 1 John 1-10. How does the first verse serve as a thematic topic sentence for the passage?

In both the NIV and ESV, there is a clause tacked on to the end of the verse. What is it? What purpose does it serve?

How does your understanding of adoption help you connect to this verse?

WEEK 3, DAY 5
How God Sees You: Reflection

Write 1 John 3:1 here

In the passage for the week, John is writing to fellow believers, those who have accepted in faith the work done by Christ on the cross. They had been reconciled to God because someone else took the punishment they deserved. Where do you stand in your own reconciliation with God?

How has your understanding of God's view of you changed this week?

Who in your life needs to hear about God's adoption of his children who have come to faith?

WEEK 4, DAY 1
Fervor and Futility

The ER nurse, the one who had just hooked me up to an EKG, quipped, "You just need to relax." I was in the middle of my second major panic attack, and I was terrified. Her cold advice was not only unhelpful but impossible to follow.

Why impossible? I was in spiritual bondage. In three years, I had been through eleven supervisors, and with each one, I had worked harder and harder to please, to prove myself, to show myself capable and smart. Each person was entirely new to my department, so I *had* to work—consciously and subconsciously—to figure out what impressed each one. I was a servant and slave to my own need for approval. I worked really hard to forge the links in that chain, even to the point of "dropping in" to my principal's office on days so that he could see I was working late. I volunteered when I didn't have time to so that I could look like a team player. I was a scheduling martyr when I took the class that no one else wanted.

The result? I exhausted myself trying to read the minds of my peers and influence the way they thought.

A good friend said, "Angie, you cannot make another person see you a particular way. You cannot create someone else's opinion of you." *So, if I cannot make another person approve of me, why am I working so hard to do so? When I can choose not to work to impress, the bondage will be broken.*

Here's the tough part: How do we get free from bondage? Is it a work solely of the Holy Spirit, or a work of my will? Is it a matter of choice or simple submission to God? Yes to all of these. I think it looks like this: I confess to God my sin of working to please others instead of him, ask for the filling of the Holy Spirit to empower me to choose freedom, look for opportunities to leave the chains behind, and act. THE RESULT WILL BE FREEDOM FROM BONDAGE. That doesn't mean we can't start re-forging the links and wrapping that chain back around our feet, so this process is an ongoing one.

WEEK 4, DAY 2
Fervor and Futility: Breaking Free

In the chart below, list some responsibilities you have taken on that may be tied to pleasing others rather than God. You might also list some chronic behaviors or habits. Pray that God would reveal your motives to you.

Responsibility/Behavior	Motive
Leadership team chair	I wanted to impress my principal.

Pay attention today to your choices. When an opportunity arises for you to toot your own horn, don't do it. If you have the chance to tell a story that makes you look capable, smart, organized, or creative, keep it to yourself. At the end of the day, make some notes here about the experiences.

WEEK 4, DAY 3
Fervor and Futility: Scripture Memorization

Galatians 1:10

ESV
For am I now seeking the approval of man, or of God? Or am I trying to please man? If I were still trying to please man, I would not be a servant of Christ.

NIV
Am I now trying to win the approval of human beings, or of God? Or am I trying to please people? If I were still trying to please people, I would not be a servant of Christ.

KJV
For do I now persuade men, or God? or do I seek to please men? for if I yet pleased men, I should not be the servant of Christ.

Choose one version of the verse above and write it here.

Create an image that will help you remember the major concepts of the verse.

WEEK 4, DAY 4
Fervor and Futility: Scripture Study

Write Galatians 1:10 here.

Historical Context

The Apostle Paul included these lines in a letter to the church at Galatia, which included both Jewish and Gentile converts. The new followers had begun to muddy the waters, mixing the Gospel (grace alone) with Mosaic Law in the belief that both were necessary for salvation. They were even requiring Gentile converts to follow Jewish traditions. Chapter 1 warns the group not to stray from the pure Gospel.

In the context of Chapter 1, why do you think Paul uses two rhetorical questions in this verse?

Put the "If" statement in your own words.

How does this verse apply to your life?

WEEK 4, DAY 5
Fervor and Futility: Reflection

Write Galatians 1:10 here.

What sin has the Holy Spirit revealed to you this week?

Briefly recount an experience when you felt conviction or a reminder from the Holy Spirit. You might consider this a "pricking" of the Spirit or the hearing of the small, still voice.

Briefly recount a circumstance in which you chose not to act out of a desire to please or impress another person. Did it feel freeing or stifling?

Stop now and pray, thanking God for his work in you, confessing any sin revealed to you, and asking God to continue to refine you in this area

WEEK 5, DAY 1
Blessed Discomfort

If braces don't cause pain, they aren't working. If a first kiss isn't a little awkward and goofy, it's probably not memorable. If we don't sweat, we're not getting much from a workout. You learn to trust a friend by putting yourself out there, telling a secret you hope he'll keep.

A relationship with God involves all these things—pain, awkwardness, work, and risk. Risk may be the toughest one. If your life does not require you to do uncomfortable things, you will never see your need for God.

What could this look like? You're chatting with a co-worker on a workday, and you sense the Holy Spirit's prompting to say something specific or to explain the Gospel. Without thinking through all the ramifications of speaking up, analyzing the risk of losing this person's approval, or wondering if you'll make your meeting if the conversation takes off, you just open your mouth and speak.

God does not call us to the results of our obedience, just the obedience. We don't know how the person has been prepared for the conversation, what life events have transpired to soften the person to hear what you have to say, how close that person is to conversion, or what will happen tomorrow that will necessitate the person's recall of what you said. The context is God's.

Each time we act in faith that God has the big picture, we trust him a bit more. That does not mean we should take unnecessary risks—like handling snakes or base jumping—in order to prove to ourselves and others that God will protect us. It does mean, however, that we can't stay comfortable and safe.

WEEK 5, DAY 2
Blessed Discomfort: Taking a Risk

Which of these actions creates or would probably create major discomfort for you? Check as many as you like.

☐ Talking to a family member about Jesus

☐ Taking an unpopular public stand against something unethical or immoral

☐ Acknowledging to your staff your relationship with God through Jesus Christ

☐ Speaking to a homeless person

☐ Telling a co-worker about something God has done in your life

☐ Crossing cultures locally to serve others in the name of Christ

☐ Giving food, clothing, or water to a student who is obviously in need

Choose one of the items you checked. What is the *worst* thing that could happen if you chose to take this risk for Jesus? If you like, list all the possible consequences of doing this thing.

If the possible consequences are holding you back, that is fear. Acting or abstaining out of fear is a limiting way to live. What are some possible positive results of doing this thing? (It's likely that the outcome is nothing you would expect. God loves surprises.)

We are called to do everything on this list. Carrying out these tasks does not save us or make God love us more; however, we are the workers, and there is work to be done to communicate God's love to a desperate, dying world. Remember that the context is God's. The equipping is God's to do. We are not responsible for creating any specific outcome. So, take one step this week. Do that one thing you wrote about for the question above.

WEEK 5, DAY 3

Blessed Discomfort: Scripture Memorization

1 Thessalonians 5:24

NIV
The one who calls you is faithful, and he will do it.

CEV
The one who chose you can be trusted, and he will do this.

KJV
Faithful *is* he that calleth you, who also will do *it*.

Choose one version of the verse above and write it here.

WEEK 5, DAY 4

Blessed Discomfort: Scripture Study

Write 1 Thessalonians 5:24 here.

Context

Paul and Silas traveled together to Thessalonica and preached for three weeks in the synagogue. The two men led many to Christ, including some prominent women. Both Greeks and Jews converted. Paul's first letter to these believers, specifically what has become the fifth chapter, is about the coming of Christ and the Godly treatment of each other as members of a community.

Read all of 1 Thessalonians 5. Take a look at verses 23 and 24 together:

23 May God himself, the God of peace, sanctify you through and through. May your whole spirit, soul and body be kept blameless at the coming of our Lord Jesus Christ.
24 The one who calls you is faithful, and he will do it.

Who is "the one" in verse 24?

To what does he "call" us (or the recipients of this letter)?

Within the context of your school, to what does he call you?

WEEK 5, DAY 5
Blessed Discomfort: Reflection

Write 1 Thessalonians 5:24 here.

How did it feel to *contemplate* stepping out of your comfort zone this week?

If you did confront fear with faith by acting on one of the Day 2 tasks, what were the results? Be sure to include emotional, spiritual, relational, and even professional results.

While God's character is consistent, he is wonderfully creative. What surprises did you experience this week?

WEEK 6, DAY 1
Speaking Life

Picture the face of a teacher you didn't like or one who didn't seem to like you very much. Now try to recall his or her voice. It's stuck in your head, isn't it? You can probably picture some outfits the teacher wore, and you might even remember perfume, cologne, the stench of cigarettes, or the smell of breath mints. *All of your senses* remember that teacher. Equally, you can name the teacher who spoke life into you, encouraged you, or inspired you. I can recount every line in the face of my seventh-grade language arts teacher, who told me I was too emotionally immature to be gifted. But I can also spot the shade of red Patsy Wright used on her fingernails when I was in the tenth grade. She handed me a stack of papers and said, "You're a really good writer. Here are some contests I want you to enter." (In 2015, my mother called me from a doctor's office to tell me that Mrs. Wright was sitting beside her in the waiting room. Mom handed her the phone, and I got to tell her that I'm still writing.)

- "Why do you cry so much? You're too sensitive."
  Mrs. S, Grade 7, 1981, striped polyester shirts
- "You can take your pick. We're fighting over you! Mrs. O wants you in chorus, Mrs. B wants you for yearbook, and I want you in drama."
  Mr. W, Grade 9, 1983, khaki pants and plaid buttoned shirts
- "Three times four is *NOT* seven! *WHY* are you so careless?"
  Every math teacher, every grade, 1974-1986, grumpy faces

We can speak life or death into the spirits of our students. Scripture says the tongue can be a "honeycomb" or "deadly poison" (Proverbs 16:24; James 3:8). It can be a "tree of life," or it can bring "fire" (Proverbs 15:4; James 3:6).

WEEK 6, DAY 2
Speaking Life: Living it Out

There are students who remember you because you loved them well or taught them well. There is also at least one student out there whom you hurt, perhaps deeply. What's his or her name? What do you recall about the pain you may have caused this student?

Confess your sin aloud to the Lord and accept his forgiveness.

You currently have students who are difficult to love, like, or even tolerate. Write their initials below. Plan ways you can speak life to them this week.

WEEK 6, DAY 3
Speaking Life: Scripture Memorization

Proverbs 16:24

NIV

Gracious words are a honeycomb, sweet to the soul and healing to the bones.

ESV

Gracious words are like a honeycomb, sweetness to the soul and health to the body.

KJV

Pleasant words are as an honeycomb, sweet to the soul, and health to the bones.

Choose one version of the verse above and write it here.

WEEK 6, DAY 4
Speaking Life: Scripture Study

Write Proverbs 16:24 here.

Context

The probable author of this chapter of Proverbs is King Solomon, who was known for his wisdom.

There are eight references to honeycombs in the canonized Old Testament. Read through these verses and make notes on the right about the way the honeycomb idea is used metaphorically in the Bible.

- 1st Samuel 14:27

- Psalms 19:10

- Proverbs 5:3

- Proverbs 16:24

- Proverbs 24:13

- Proverbs 27:7

- Song of Solomon 4:11

- Song of Solomon 5:1

What are "gracious words?"

In light of the honeycomb metaphor, how powerful are they?

WEEK 6, DAY 5
Speaking Life: Reflection

Write Proverbs 16:24 here.

There is a time to be blunt and perhaps even harsh, but in a school setting, that mode of operation doesn't work very well. Briefly describe below a time this week when you held back to avoid hurting a student, peer, or parent. Explain why you do or do not have any regrets about your decision to change your tone or approach.

Briefly recount a time this week when you intentionally spoke life to someone.

Just like stepping out in faith requires that we release the control of results, so does speaking life. Can you deal with someone who reacts negatively or neutrally toward a kind word from you?

WEEK 7, DAY I
Hearing God's Voice

There are a lot of voices coming at us. A believer hears from other Christians, our culture via social media and television, the subculture of educators and researchers, our families, our enemy, and the Holy Spirit. How do we know which one to listen to and which ones to filter?

All truth is God's truth. If what a researcher discovers lines up with biblical scripture, it's true. You could create a two-foot stack of studies touting the power of constructive criticism. The Apostle Paul wrote about "speaking the truth in love" to the church at Ephesus. If what social media feeds you does not line up, it's false. For example, the American culture's norm is for a person to have car loans, student loans, *and* a mortgage; but the Bible is loud and clear about the dangers of debt. It even calls the borrower a "slave to the lender" (Proverbs 22:7).

We must "test the spirits to see if they are from God" (1 John 4:1). Hold them up to the light so that you can see through them. Is the message you are hearing true? Honorable? Just? Pure? Lovely? Commendable? Worthy of praise? (Philippians 4:8). Are you hearing it from someone who is loving, joyful, peaceful, patient, kind, good, faithful, gentle, and in control of himself or herself? (Galatians 5:22-23). On the other hand, filter out the advice from people who are known for being sexually immoral, stirring up conflict, having a short or raging temper, and drinking too much (Galatians 5:19).

Most importantly, know God's voice so well that when you hear it, you know it. There are two main ways to learn the voice of God: studying his Word and listening to him in prayer. The United States Secret Service trains its agents to spot counterfeit money by having them study the real thing. They *never* look at counterfeit bills in training. By knowing every line, curve, color, and texture of the real, they are able to spot the fake.

The job of Satan is to lie, steal, kill, and destroy. He's out for blood, and he's not stupid. A subtle lie, an almost-truth, is his main weapon. Know how to spot one.

WEEK 7, DAY 2
Hearing God's Voice: Living it Out

What voices do you avoid? For example, do you stay away from certain types of books or movies, certain social media outlets, etc.?

What voices do you find attractive or hard to resist? For example, do you find your family members' opinions of your choices important?

Have you ever struggled to figure out the will of God? What did that look like for you? Loss of sleep? Tears? Seeking of advice?

Think through your own process of seeking to understand God and what he wants for your life. Describe it below.

WEEK 7, DAY 3
Hearing God's Voice: Scripture Memorization

Romans 12:2

NIV
Do not conform to the pattern of this world, but be transformed by the renewing of your mind. Then you will be able to test and approve what God's will is—his good, pleasing and perfect will.

ESV
Do not be conformed to this world, but be transformed by the renewal of your mind, that by testing you may discern what is the will of God, what is good and acceptable and perfect.

KJV
And be not conformed to this world: but be ye transformed by the renewing of your mind, that ye may prove what is that good, and acceptable, and perfect, will of God.

Choose one version of the verse above and write it here.

Memorization Tip:

Divide this verse into clauses and learn them in chunks.

WEEK 7, DAY 4
Hearing God's Voice: Scripture Study

Write Romans 12:2 here.

What is required for a believer to be able to "test and approve what God's will is" (NIV)?

What does it mean not to conform to the world?

What is the "renewing" of your mind?

What would it look like not to conform to the "pattern" at school?

WEEK 7, DAY 5
Hearing God's Voice: Reflection

You may have realized this week that you're exposing yourself to voices you need to avoid. Consider this list of sources. Where do you need to limit exposure?

Family members
Movies
News
Friends
Television
Co-workers
Novels
Political articles
Other

You may also have realized this week that you need to do more listening. Consider this list of sources. From which sources do you need to increase intake?

Bible
Prayer
Sermons
Fellowship with believers
Christian books
Christian podcasts, videos, etc.
Other

What in particular stuck with you this week from this set of readings and materials?

WEEK 8, DAY 1
Armor Up

The typical tour of duty during The Vietnam Conflict was twelve months. That's 365 days of being on edge, in a place a man never meant to be, often without support from home. The slow trauma of being stalked by a stealthy unseen enemy wore a man down, broke him, or killed him.

A traditional American school year lasts ten months. That's 180 days of being scrutinized, evaluated, watched, held to impossible standards. Lesson plans and assessments have to be written. Parents must be satisfied. The pressure crushes us.

Then we come back for another tour of duty. And another. And another. And another. We see desks and white boards and bins and lockers, but on another plane, there are swords clashing over our heads and arrows whizzing past them. You hear a clock ticking during a test, but there are also battle cries being screamed across the room.

Don't be fooled: Whether or not you believe something to be true does not change its truth. There are some principles that just *are*, and one of them is that God is good. Another? You have an enemy whose sole purpose is to make you forget that God is good.

Being a teacher is no joke. There is barbed wire between those rows of desks, trip wire in the hallway, and razor wire across the board. You are on the front lines of a battle for children, for co-workers, and for yourself. Don't go into battle wearing a cute denim jumper. Armor up!

WEEK 8, DAY 2
Armor Up: Living it Out

Whether you have 22 second graders who are with you all day every day or 150 teenagers who cycle through your room over the course of six periods, each one needs prayer. Grab your seating chart and class roster(s) and get to it. Your perspective of each child as both a creation and a target just may change.

How to pray:

- You might sit in each desk and pray specifically by name for each child who sits there.

- Thank God for some specific attribute of that child or something the Lord has brought her through.

- Intercede on behalf of that student for protection and a vibrant relationship with God through Christ. Add anything else that's on your mind—wisdom in relationships, academic success, etc.

Write below and on the next page any realizations you had while praying. The Holy Spirit may have softened your heart toward a troublemaker, made a connection between behavior and home life, or given you a word of knowledge that could only come from God.

WEEK 8, DAY 3
Armor Up: Scripture Memorization

Ephesians 6:10-18 NIV

Finally, be strong in the Lord and in his mighty power. Put on the full armor of God, so that you can take your stand against the devil's schemes. For our struggle is not against flesh and blood, but against the rulers, against the authorities, against the powers of this dark world and against the spiritual forces of evil in the heavenly realms. Therefore put on the full armor of God, so that when the day of evil comes, you may be able to stand your ground, and after you have done everything, to stand. Stand firm then, with the belt of truth buckled around your waist, with the breastplate of righteousness in place, and with your feet fitted with the readiness that comes from the gospel of peace. In addition to all this, take up the shield of faith, with which you can extinguish all the flaming arrows of the evil one. Take the helmet of salvation and the sword of the Spirit, which is the word of God. And pray in the Spirit on all occasions with all kinds of prayers and requests. With this in mind, be alert and always keep on praying for all the Lord's people.

If you enjoy memorization, you might want to tackle this entire passage. Otherwise, consider choosing verses 11 and 12. Write below the verses you decide to learn in the version of your choice.

WEEK 8, DAY 4
Armor Up: Scripture Study

Write below Ephesians 6:11-12 or the verses you are learning.

Context

Ephesus, in what is now modern Turkey, was a port city and part of the Roman Empire. Paul's letter was most likely distributed to other churches from there. Most scholars agree that Paul wrote this letter when he was imprisoned in Rome, so he would have had fully dressed Roman soldiers around him for observation and study; thus, he is able to go into detail about their uniform. His audience(s) would also be familiar with the uniform.

Paul discusses six pieces of armor. List them and then put into your own words what it would look like practically to put on this metaphorical piece of equipment.

Paul leaves the extended metaphor to add prayer to the end of the list of weapons we are to use. What could be his reason for doing so?

WEEK 8, DAY 5
Armor Up: Reflection

Write below Ephesians 6:11-12 or the verses you are learning.

Define spiritual warfare.

Do you generally think of your job as a battleground? Why or why not?

Briefly describe an incident or relationship that bears the marks of Satan's work in your school.

List again the weapons you have against the enemy.

What habits do you need to develop in order to be fully armed?

WEEK 9, DAY 1
Perfectionism and Gas Pedals

In the video series that accompanies *The Armor of God,* Priscilla Shirer drops a powerful truth bomb: *Perfectionism is insecurity in an art form.* In a school setting, perfectionism stands out. It looks like the teacher who gets to work at 7:00 and leaves at 6:00. It's that car sitting in the parking lot on a Sunday. It's the planning-period conversation criticizing the young teacher who gets to work on time, leaves on time, and doesn't take work home.

Often the time and effort put into school is an attempt to be the *most* hard-working, *most* rigorous, even the *most* exhausted, as if the bags under my eyes are a badge of honor. It's all about comparison, right? Compared to the one next door who shows movies all the time, I'm doing ok. Compared to the one who spends thirty minutes on each essay, I suck. I'm either smart, confident, and accomplished; or I'm inferior, weak, and lowly. King Solomon saw it: "And I saw that all toil and all achievement spring from one person's envy of another. This too is meaningless, a chasing after the wind" (Ecclesiastes 4:4-6).

David Mallard, an excellent friend and former pastor, used to say, "If Satan can't get your foot off the gas pedal, he'll just press it down harder." Our work for the Kingdom of God, in the form of being part of a school community, is driven by what he has called us to do—no more, no less. We are to take his yoke upon us, a burden no oxen is ever asked to bear alone. Each ox is placed in the yoke, and the two are side by side, sharing the weight and the work (Matthew 11:29). When one ox tries to pull ahead of the other, there's discomfort, even pain, and the work slows down.

We are indeed called to work as unto the Lord (Colossians 3:23), but we are not called to exhaust ourselves doing it. School culture has set us up for fatigue, and we have to resist the compulsion to work hard just for the sake of working hard.

When a plane loses pressure, passengers are told to use the oxygen masks on themselves first before helping someone else. It's not selfishness that demands that we care for ourselves first; it's about being around so that we *can* help someone else.

WEEK 9, DAY 2
Perfectionism and Gas Pedals: Living it Out

What's the difference between mediocrity and work-life balance?

Can you handle being average? Do you have to be the *most effective* administrator, *most beloved* teacher, or *most respected* curriculum specialist?

Here's your challenge: Pick one day this week when you will leave work empty handed—no papers to grade, no lessons to write, no spreadsheets to fill out, no work-related phone calls to make. Leave school with your coat, purse, or lunch bag, and that's it. When you get home, don't talk about school. Just live in your first name. Come back here once you complete the challenge and write about it on the next page.

What did you have to change in order to make it work?

Did you change your time management (come in early, work through lunch, stay late)?

Did you miss a deadline or return student work later than you generally would?

Did the world implode? If not, what consequences or benefits did you experience?

WEEK 9, DAY 3
Perfectionism and Gas Pedals

Colossians 3:23-24

ESV
Whatever you do, work heartily, as for the Lord and not for men, knowing that from the Lord you will receive the inheritance as your reward. You are serving the Lord Christ.

ISV
Whatever you do, work at it wholeheartedly as though you were doing it for the Lord and not merely for people. You know that it is from the Lord that you will receive the inheritance as a reward. It is the Lord Messiah whom you are serving!

KJV
And whatsoever ye do, do *it* heartily, as to the Lord, and not unto men; Knowing that of the Lord ye shall receive the reward of the inheritance: for ye serve the Lord Christ.

Choose one version of the verse above and write it here.

Memorization Tip

For this verse, cut out the memory card and tape it to your school computer.

WEEK 9, DAY 4
Perfectionism and Gas Pedals: Scripture Study

Write Colossians 3:23-24 below.

Context
The Apostle Paul wrote this letter to the church at Colossae, but there is no evidence that he ever actually visited this group of Gentile believers. He addresses a false teaching that was permeating the group— referred to by modern scholars as the "Colossian heresy"—but the exact nature of the teaching is disputed.

What two active verbs does Paul use in this verse?

How do you read the inheritance idea in the passage?

What is the inheritance?

Does God reward us for our work, or are we to work in the knowledge that we will be receiving the reward of inheritance?

At school, where is the line between working "heartily" or "wholeheartedly" and working "for men?"

WEEK 9, DAY 5
Perfectionism and Gas Pedals: Reflection

Write Colossians 3:23-24 below.

Use the chart below to list traits of a teacher, administrator, or curriculum coach who is weak, effective, and over-the-top perfectionistic.

Weak	Effective	Over the Top

Where do you fall in the chart?

What needs to change in order for you to strike a balance between working hard for the Lord and working hard for other reasons?

WEEK 10, DAY 1
Unplugging Shame

She was Black and terrified. A woman in her late 40s held tight to the rails of the stairs leading into the pool. As I came to the end of a lap and stood to rest, I watched her put two adult life vests around her large torso before gripping her way into the water.

In the pool were 60 white senior citizens doing water aerobics together. They stood huddled in small groups, talking, jogging in place, and using their foam hand weights, completely unaware that bondage was being broken right behind them.

Understand what happened. In the *rural South*, a *Black woman* who was *terrified of water* got into a *swimming pool* full of *older white people*. Not only that, but she was heavy, and she showed her body. What courage!

Beyond guilt, beyond conviction, beyond embarrassment, beyond even emotion, shame is a surety that we are *less than-because of*. It operates on the belief that we should keep hidden away something we have done or something we are. It drives abortions, the pornography industry, and swimsuit design. Whereas embarrassment might be incidental, shame is *entrenched* and must be dug out.

Shame and fear work well together; one thrives on experienced pain, and the other thrives on anticipated pain. While some struggles can be dealt with through avoidance, these two don't work that way. They have to be approached, entered into, felt, and left behind.

What does it look like to leave shame behind? It's the girl who can joke about having free lunch. It's the boy who comes before school to tell you he doesn't understand what you're teaching. It's the first-year teacher who tells everyone at a grade-level meeting that she came into the job wholly unprepared and needs help planning her lessons.

A person who leaves shame behind is humble, teachable, and most importantly, free.

WEEK 10, DAY 2
Unplugging Shame: Living it Out

Write down your own definition of shame.

List two areas in which you live in shame instead of freedom.

What would it look like to move from shame to freedom?

In what ways do we impose shame on our students and co-workers?

Make ONE choice this week to free yourself, a student, or a co-worker from shame. Come back and write an account of the experience here.

WEEK 10, DAY 3
Unplugging Shame: Scripture Memorization

Malachi 4:2

NIV

But for you who revere my name, the sun of righteousness will rise with healing in its rays. And you will go out and frolic like well-fed calves.

NASB

But for you who fear My name, the sun of righteousness will rise with healing in its wings; and you will go forth and skip about like calves from the stall.

RSV

But for you who fear my name the sun of righteousness shall rise, with healing in its wings. You shall go forth leaping like calves from the stall.

KJV

But unto you that fear my name shall the Sun of righteousness arise with healing in his wings; and ye shall go forth, and grow up as calves of the stall.

Choose one version of the verse above and write it here.

WEEK 10, DAY 4
Unplugging Shame: Scripture Study

Write Malachi 4:2 here.

Context

Malachi is a prophetic book found at the end of the Old Testament. Probably written in the fifth century B.C. after the Jews were freed from captivity in Babylon, it points the Israelites to the love of God, the need for obedience, and the coming of the Messiah.

Language

Look back at the four versions of this verse provided in Day 3. Write down the four verbs used to depict the behavior of the calves.

NIV: _____

NAS: _____

RSV: _____

KJV: _____

What do these words/phrases have in common?

Who are the calves in the simile?

How might this verse apply to shame?

WEEK 10, DAY 5
Unplugging Shame: Reflection

Write Malachi 4:2 here.

How has your understanding of shame developed this week?

Pray and ask the Holy Spirit to reveal any areas in which you need to move out of shame into freedom. Make notes here as you listen.

Pray and ask the Holy Spirit to reveal ways you shame your family, students, and co-workers. Make notes here as you confess and experience God's forgiveness.

WEEK II, DAY I
Vulnerability

I started teaching in 1990, and we always dressed professionally—dress, slip, hose, makeup, jewelry. And high heels. When students heard clicking in the hall, they knew a teacher was walking by. Mine used to tell me I had a distinctive "click, scrape" that warned them I was coming. That "click, scrape" once allowed my heel to catch on a loose tile and send me literally bouncing down an entire flight of steps. When I landed, I was on my hands and knees (sans shoes) staring at the sneakers of two seniors. The hem of my dress was somewhere in the vicinity of my waist. By the time the students handed me my shoes, everyone knew. I think there was some sort of communication system in the bricks. Those two students saw me—all of me—at my worst, but by the end of the day, I was telling the story myself (although it hurt to laugh).

People have told me throughout my career that I seem to have it together. It's not true. I am a hot mess about 98% of the time. My home is chaotic, my car looks and smells like the floor of a movie theater, I bounce checks regularly just because I don't pay attention, and my phone is never charged. Now you know. My students know too. I let them see the hotness of the mess. When I lose my temper—which is frequent—I apologize. When I need their grace during times of personal struggle, I ask for it.

Our students need to see our human-ness. We may need to act like we've got it going on for the first few weeks of school, but after that, let loose the bun. Even the Apostle Paul kept his pedestal low in writing to the brand-new believers around the Mediterranean; he admitted to wrestling with sin and doing the very things he didn't want to do.

Author Jennie Allen writes in *Anything*, "There is something to humility that is costly . . . something resembling humiliation . . . an outright declaration of the wreck we are without God rather than composing a beautiful existence that barely needs a savior" (15).

As an educator, you may be the best reader, artist, or mathematician in the room; but you must not consider yourself the beacon of morality. It's important for students to see you make good choices, but they also need to see the ugly ones and the repentance that follows them.

WEEK 11, DAY 2
Vulnerability: Living it Out

Briefly recount a time when you lost your temper or did something wrong in front of students. How did they react? How did you react?

How important is it to you that students perceive you as having it together?

What would it look like to be vulnerable with your peers?

What are the risks involved in being vulnerable with your superiors? With parents? What can you imagine that God could do in you when you take those kinds of risks?

WEEK 11, DAY 3
Vulnerability: Scripture Memorization

John 3:30

NIV

He must become greater; I must become less.

ESV

He must increase, but I must decrease.

KJV

He must increase, but I must decrease.

Choose one version of the verse above and write it here.

WEEK II, DAY 4
Vulnerability: Scripture Study

Write John 3:30 below.

Context

The Apostle John is quoting John the Baptist in this passage. John the Baptist, Jesus' cousin and the prophet announcing the arrival of the Messiah, is using an extended wedding metaphor in response to a question from "a certain Jew" about the fact that Jesus is baptizing just across the river Jordan. John the Baptist had been preaching repentance and baptizing, and there is concern that Jesus has taken his place.

Read John 3:22-30 in its entirety.

Who (literally) are the characters in the extended metaphor John the Baptist is using?

Who (metaphorically) do these characters represent?

What does John the Baptist mean when he says to the crowd, "He must become greater; I must become less"?

Who are *you* in this metaphor?

WEEK II, DAY 5
Vulnerability: Reflection

Write John 3:30 below.

Read again the Jennie Allen quotation from Day 1:

"There is something to humility that is costly . . . something resembling humiliation . . . an outright declaration of the wreck we are without God rather than composing a beautiful existence that barely needs a savior" (15).

Stop now and pray through these three questions:

> **Do you compose "a beautiful existence that barely needs a savior?"**

> **Is it possible that your "togetherness" is getting in the way of God working through to you to bring someone to faith in Christ?**

Who needs to see your vulnerability?

WEEK 12, DAY 1
The Rip Tide of Dissent

High school English teachers have a reputation for being grouchy, critical curmudgeons. We all metaphorically have hair buns and reading glasses at the end of our noses, over which we can stare at students like they just split an infinitive. Want to snicker cynically in the back row at a staff meeting? Sit next to an English teacher.

Complaint and discontent look like a harmless eddies in a stream, swirling, catching up dead leaves and broken sticks, but the pull to be just as cynical is like a rip tide. We are pulled and carried along until we realize how hard it is to get out. Teaching is hard, but we can make it harder by wallowing in the parts of it that are unfair and exhausting.

Compare versions of Proverbs 16:28, and you'll find that a person who causes strife or conflict is called perverse, destructive, wicked, and deceitful. He is miserable, and he wants everyone else to be miserable too.

This deadly, drowning rip tide is no place for a follower of Christ.

Paul urges us in Hebrews 10:24-25 "to stir up one another to love and good works, not neglecting to meet together, as is the habit of some, but encouraging one another, and all the more as you see the Day drawing near" (ESV). That doesn't sound like what happens in the teachers' lounge.

Stay away from it. When it starts happening, swim hard. Keep your head above the water with a change of topic, a counter statement, an encouraging word, a different perspective, or an exit from the conversation. You might be called Pollyanna. You might be considered aloof. You might even be lonely, but whining with the whiner will not point that person to God.

WEEK 12, DAY 2
The Rip Tide of Dissent: Living it Out

Could you name the cynics, whiners, and curmudgeons at your school? (You don't need to write anything; just picture them.) Do you find yourself drawn to them in any way?

How hard is it to walk away, change the topic, or contradict what they are saying?

Are *you* the cynical, whining curmudgeon? Do you find yourself looking for things to complain about? Do you notice that new teachers find it hard to step away from your diatribes? Stop and pray now. Confess your sin and ask for God's empowerment to practice self control as you begin changing this habit.

What's the difference between appropriate dissent and simple complaint?

When would dissent be called for in the school setting?

WEEK 12, DAY 3
The Rip Tide of Dissent: Scripture Memorization

Galatians 5:19-21

NIV

The acts of the flesh are obvious: sexual immorality, impurity and debauchery; idolatry and witchcraft; hatred, discord, jealousy, fits of rage, selfish ambition, dissensions, factions and envy; drunkenness, orgies, and the like. I warn you, as I did before, that those who live like this will not inherit the kingdom of God.

ESV

Now the works of the flesh are evident: sexual immorality, impurity, sensuality, idolatry, sorcery, enmity, strife, jealousy, fits of anger, rivalries, dissensions, divisions, envy, drunkenness, orgies, and things like these. I warn you, as I warned you before, that those who do such things will not inherit the kingdom of God.

KJV

Now the works of the flesh are manifest, which are these; adultery, fornication, uncleanness, lasciviousness, idolatry, witchcraft, hatred, variance, emulations, wrath, strife, seditions, heresies, envyings, murders, drunkenness, revellings, and such like: of the which I tell you before, as I have also told you in time past, that they which do such things shall not inherit the kingdom of God.

Choose one version of the verse and write it here.

WEEK 12, DAY 4
The Rip Tide of Dissent: Scripture Study

Write below Galatians 5:19-21

List below as many of the acts of the flesh as you can recall from your work with the verse on Day 3.

What conclusions can you draw about the struggles of the church at Galatia?

Circle or rewrite the sins listed that relate to *stirring up discontent*.

How does this scripture apply to your work as an educator?

WEEK 12, DAY 5
The Rip Tide of Dissent: Reflection

Write below Galatians 5:19-21

While doing this week's exercises, what have you noticed about the educators around you? Who in your school seems to stay above it all?

Have you experienced the Holy Spirit's conviction this week? If so, in what circumstance(s)?

Briefly recount one instance in which you were able to escape a rip tide.

ABOUT THE AUTHOR

Angie is a high school English teacher, curriculum designer, speaker, and professional development trainer in central North Carolina, where she lives with her husband and son. You can find her at angiekratzer.com.

Photo by Marcella Storie Photography

Works Consulted

Allen, Jennie. *Anything: The Prayer That Unlocked My God and My Soul*. Nashville, Tennessee: W Publishing, 2011. Print.

Bhanoo, Sindya N. "A Colorful Crustacean with a Knockout Punch." nytimes.com. 11 Jun. 2012. Web. 19 Jul. 2016.

"Bible Concordance: 'honeycomb.'" learnthebible.org. 2001-2016. Web. 25 Jul. 2016.

"Bible Study Guide: 1 John, 2 John, 3 John." americanbible.org. American Bible Society. 2016. Web. 25 Jul. 2016.

Chan, Francis. *Crazy Love: Overwhelmed by a Relentless God*. Colorado Springs: David C. Cook, 2013. Print.

Contemporary English Version. Bible Gateway. Web. 25 Jul. 2016.

English Standard Version. Bible Gateway. Web. 20 Jul. 2016.

Harris, W. Hall III. "The Authorship of 1 John." Bible.org. 2016. Web. 24 Jul. 2016.

Henry, Matthew. *Matthew Henry Commentary on the Whole Bible (Complete): Psalms 27*. Biblestudytools.com. 2014. Web. 21 Jun. 2016.

Herrick, Greg, Ph.D. "The Book of Ephesians." Bible.org. 18 Aug.

    2004. Web. 20 Jul. 2016. *International Standard Version.* Bible

    Gateway. Web. 18 Jul. 2016.

Keathley, J. Hampton III. "Background on Colossians." Bible.org. 1

    Jul. 2004. Web. 28 Jul. 2016.

King James Version. Bible Gateway. Web. 20 Jul. 2016.

Malick, David. "An Introduction to First Thessalonians." Bible.org.

    2016. Web. 26 July 2016.

New American Standard Bible. Bible Gateway. Web. 19 Jul. 2016.

New International Version. Bible Gateway. Web. 20 Jul. 2016.

Peach, David. "Romans 12: Bible Study and Summary."

    whatchristianswantoknow.com. Telling Ministries Inc. 2010-

    2016. Web. 21 Jul. 2016.

Shirer, Priscilla. *The Armor of God.* Nashville, Tennessee: Lifeway,

    2015. Print.

Tully, Brent. "How Big Is the Universe?" pbs.org. WGBH

    Educational Foundation. 11 Nov. 2000. Web. 19 Jul. 2016.

"What is a galaxy?" spaceplace.nasa.gov. NASA. 19 Jul. 2016. Web.

    19 Jul. 2016.

SCRIPTURE MEMORY CARDS

Week 1   **Psalm 27:14**   NIV

Wait for the LORD; be strong and take heart and wait for the LORD.

Week 2   **Romans 3:23-25a**   NIV

[. . .] for all have sinned and fall short of the glory of God, and all are justified freely by his grace through the redemption that came by Christ Jesus. God presented Christ as a sacrifice of atonement, through the shedding of his blood—to be received by faith.

BACK OF SCRIPTURE MEMORY CARDS FOR WEEKS 3 AND 4

Week 3 **1 John 3:1** ESV

See what kind of love the Father has given to us, that we should be called children of God; and so we are.

Week 4 **Galatians 1:10** NIV

Am I now trying to win the approval of human beings, or of God? Or am I trying to please people? If I were still trying to please people, I would not be a servant of Christ.

BACK OF SCRIPTURE MEMORY CARDS FOR WEEKS 5, 6, AND 7

Week 5   **1 Thess. 5:24**   NIV

The one who calls you is faithful, and he will do it.

Week 6   **Proverbs 16:24**   NIV

Gracious words are a honeycomb, sweet to the soul and healing to the bones.

Week 7   **Romans 12:2**   NIV

Do not conform to the pattern of this world, but be transformed by the renewing of your mind. Then you will be able to test and approve what God's will is—his good, pleasing and perfect will.

BACK OF SCRIPTURE MEMORY CARDS FOR WEEKS 8 AND 9

Week 8   Romans 6:11-12   NIV

Put on the full armor of God, so that you can take your stand against the devil's schemes. For our struggle is not against flesh and blood, but against the rulers, against the powers of this dark world and against the spiritual forces of evil in the heavenly realms.

Week 9   Col. 3:23-24   ESV

Whatever you do, work heartily, as for the Lord and not for men, knowing that from the Lord you will receive the inheritance as your reward. You are serving the Lord Christ.

BACK OF SCRIPTURE MEMORY CARDS FOR WEEKS 10 AND 11

Week 10 Malachi 4:2 NIV

But for you who revere my name, the sun of righteousness will rise with healing in its rays. And you will go out and frolic like well-fed calves.

Week 11 John 3:30 KJV

He must increase, but I must decrease.

BACK OF SCRIPTURE MEMORY CARD FOR WEEK 12

The acts of the flesh are obvious: sexual immorality, impurity and debauchery; idolatry and witchcraft; hatred, discord, jealousy, fits of rage, selfish ambition, dissensions, factions and envy; drunkenness, orgies, and the like. I warn you, as I did before, that those who live like this will not inherit the kingdom of God.